The Networking Field Guide™

Essential Social Skills for Business

KATHY CORDAY

ALCHEMY MEDIA GROUP, INC.™

The Networking Field Guide™: Essential Social Skills
for Business
Copyright © 2009 Kathy Corday. All rights reserved.

First Edition published 2010 by Alchemy Media Group, Inc.

This work is subject to copyright. All rights are reserved, whether the whole or part of the material is concerned, specifically the rights of translation, reprinting, re-use of illustrations, recitation, broadcasting, reproduction on microfilms, digital or in other ways, and storage in data banks. For any kind of use, permission of the copyright owner must be obtained.

For detailed information & special orders, contact
    Alchemy Media Group, Inc.
    858 West Armitage Avenue, #307
    Chicago, Illinois 60614
    Fax: 312-573-0913

    www.thenetworkingfieldguide.com

Cataloging-in-Publication Data is available from the Library of Congress, Washington, D.C.
                            2009913241

ISBN No. 978-0-9843897-0-4 (sc)

10 9 8 7 6 5 4 3 2 1

Printed in the United States of America

In loving memory of
John Hench and John Calloway

The Network Field Guide™

THE GOODS
(Contents)

CORDAY'S **TOP 10** TIPS	1
STARTING POINTS…	6
CORDAY'S **TOP 10** TIPS: *EXPRESSED!*	12
ARE YOU READY FOR A LITTLE MORE?	59
A FEW MORE WORDS OF WISDOM…	80
AFTER WORDS…	127
ABOUT THE AUTHOR	134

The Network Field Guide™

PRESSED FOR TIME?

Scan my Top 10 Networking Tips and put one or two of them to work.

HAVE MORE TIME TO INVEST?

Read through the highlighted sections on each topic.

Read along a bit further for examples and anecdotes to better assist your understanding.

Keep the Top 10 Tips reference card in your suit pocket or purse, for easy retrieval when you need it. Then, use it.

Success will follow. It is just that simple!

The Network Field Guide™

NETWORKING:
CORDAY'S TOP 10 TIPS

1. **SET GOALS**
   a. Have an objective in mind
   b. Keep it simple. (Ex. Plan to initiate 1 – 2 significant contacts per event)

2. **SMILE**
   a. It brightens every room, day or night
   b. Especially, when you're unsure of what to do or say

3. **BREATHE**
   a. When we breathe, we live
   b. Prevents you from appearing stiff
   c. If nervous upon entering a room, stroll slowly around the room for a few moments

4. **BE YOURSELF**
   a. As oneself, you are always 100%
   b. What brings us personal joy often creates enthusiasm with others
   c. Networking done well, being true to oneself, becomes effortless

5. MAKE EYE CONTACT
a. It's easier to do if you ask yourself, what's the color of his/her eyes?
b. Remember: every new contact is a friend waiting to be identified

6. SPEAK IN SOUND BITES
a. Be clear and concise
b. It leaves listeners wanting to hear more, not less

7. LISTEN CAREFULLY
a. Often times, it's what's said between the lines that makes all the difference

b. Observe body language and overall behavior
   c. Be aware of your surroundings and peripheral elements/distractions

8. **TAKE NOTE**
   a. Adjust yourself according to the pace of your listener
   b. Note select details on the back of a business card to spark your memory

9. **BE A TEAM PLAYER**
   a. Make the conversation an interactive experience

b. Share the spotlight

10. **FOLLOW UP!!!**
    a. Do what you say!
    b. Drop a note about an item of interest where appropriate
    c. Think connections and assist your network in making new ones

The Network Field Guide™

STARTING POINTS…

The Network Field Guide™

CHARISMA 101: SOCIAL SKILLS

CHARISMA

Regardless of your level of self-confidence, my Networking Field Guide™ will help you to network like a master.

Keep my Top 10 Tips at your fingertips, and you will always have a ready-reference for better communication and effective networking.

With a deep breath and a smile, you will quickly be on your way to making new contacts and cultivating new business relationships.

Imagine being asked to step outside of your comfort zone. Maybe it's as simple as attending a company function – a party, a meeting with top executives, or a sales outing.

Imagine having an ally, right inside your suit pocket or handbag with a menu of field-tested techniques to help you put your best foot forward.

What looked on the surface to be a test of your charismatic mettle quickly becomes an opportunity for you to sparkle and achieve another level of professional success.

Let's get to it!

SMALL STEPS: BIG REWARDS

I have created this field guide to be user-friendly: a plug-and-play pocket-passport to a host of key, relationship-initiation skills necessary for anyone who wishes to succeed in business today.

Created to be clear and concise, topics discussed here are easily outlined and referenced with a quick turn of a page.

You may read it in one sitting on an airplane, while enjoying a nice latte, or before you walk into that business event. Simplicity is the order of the day.

Navigating the waters of the business world, I have learned quite a bit about what makes networking effective. My skills have been obtained through the generous mentorship of established colleagues, friends, and, of course, trial and error.

You are looking at this guide because, like so many of us, you need to pick up a few new skills and are pressed for time.

Frankly, if I had written a huge, hard-cover volume filled with chapter after chapter of psychological theories and colorful statistic-filled charts, you would have left it on the shelf.

In fact, you have a desire to take your social skills to the next level.

You may be a bit shy, or perhaps you just want to gather new ideas, or shake off old habits of how to connect.

This guide has been written with only one goal in mind: to improve your ability to connect with the people you need to know to succeed.

CORDAY'S TOP 10 TIPS: *EXPRESSED!*

The Network Field Guide™

SET GOALS

- Have a specific objective in mind

    - Ex. To raise the visibility of your enterprise? Yourself? Or, a specific product?

    Whatever your goal, it's important that your goal be specific. By having a goal that is in line with your overall vision for yourself and your business, you will naturally be able to communicate in an honest and authentic fashion. One can always tell when someone is uncommitted to what they are saying or doing.

The proof is in the pudding, so to speak. When you make your objective meaningful to you, you make it meaningful to others.

- **Simplicity speaks volumes!**

  - You should be able to articulate your goal in 1 sentence.

  Plan to initiate 1 or 2 significant contacts per event, for example. A simple, straightforward goal is not only manageable it's doable.

SMILE

- It brightens any room, day or night

  - Ex. Everyone looks better wearing a smile.

  Smiles are the simplest way to show a positive attitude. Think of all the people you see sporting frowns and how unlikely you are to want to cross their path, even to say excuse me as you pass them on the street. Everyone's face looks better with the corners of their mouth pointed up rather than down. Consider it to be your own personal facial signature, so smile often and with confidence.

- It makes you approachable

  - Ex. Usually, the most charismatic people sport natural smiles and a slight head tilt.

  A genuine smile says you are open-minded and eager to connect. With the simple exchange of a smile, you can have an effect on a given situation or person in many ways. For example, in the office, it's a non-verbal greeting to colleagues; in a meeting it's a signal of cooperation; and in instances of a negative co-worker, it's a diffuser of animosity. Not to mention that a smile from a stranger is often just the pick-me-up someone needs to be rescued from an otherwise bad day.

- It's the best action to take when you're not sure of what to do or say

    - Ex. Someone makes an inappropriate comment or tells an insensitive joke.

Imagine that you are standing

among a circle of colleagues or potential clients who have influence over your ability to achieve your goals. Now, imagine that one of these people makes an inappropriate statement or tells an insensitive joke. Let your smile be your umbrella and protect you from any flack.

To call attention to this person's lack of tack would make you seem equally as rude. Instead, display a gentle, quiet smile without commenting one way or the other. Then, promptly change the subject. You have not only saved face, but you have shown yourself to be non-judgmental.

You can take this person aside and express your opinion of their remark at a time when they are more likely to listen.

BREATHE

- When we breathe, we live

    - Ex. Before entering a room, exhale deeply, and then inhale a full breath.

    There is magic in a fully-functioning diaphragm. Besides the obvious, breathing supplies the oxygen your body requires to live; it also helps your circulation and gives your voice better timbre. Plus, your mind functions at its best when oxygen is free-flowing, so you will be a more acute listener, a quicker thinker, and thus a

The Network Field Guide™

better conversationalist.

- Aside from the obvious, it prevents you from appearing stiff

    - Ex. Proper breathing relaxes your abdominal muscles and elongates your physique.

You can always spot the person who is breathing improperly in a crowded room: he or she is the one that looks as though they are about to be burned at the stake. It's a posture that is easily corrected simply by regularly breathing in and out through your diaphragm rather than from your chest. The resulting relaxed posture will make you feel more at ease and make connecting with those you hope to get to know that much easier.

- If nervous upon entering a room, take a slow stroll around the room

    - Ex. When breathing too heavily, the easiest way to slow your breathing is to mentally attempt to stop your heart.

Effective breathing is often

overlooked as a necessary skill for business relationships, but properly done is an asset that will continue to pay dividends in all aspects of your life. Proper breathing is a simple way to become more effective at networking and healthier at the same time.

BE YOURSELF

- As yourself, you are always operating at 100%

    - Ex. There is only one "YOU" on this planet.

    Celebrate yourself. No, it's not an invitation to a narcissistic gaze at your belly-button. It's a reminder that you are a unique and powerful individual. The way you see the world, the way you feel about what you see, and the way you react to that world is unique to you and you alone. Your strengths are many and your weaknesses not nearly as dire as you might want to believe. There is power in a well-adjusted sense of self; it exudes confidence without arrogance.

- What brings us personal joy often creates enthusiasm in others

    - Ex. Tell a brief anecdote about something that brings you joy.

I cannot tell you how many conversations that have picked up speed with a well-timed personal anecdote. Whether it is a story about the latest project hurdle that was overcome with humor or a hobby you enjoy away from work, tell it with enthusiasm and genuine authenticity and your listeners will be eating out of your hand. Why? Everyone loves enthusiasm. Your joy will wash over your listeners and that experience will bond all of you. You will give people a glimpse into the real you and they will appreciate it.

- Networking done well, being true to oneself, becomes nearly unnoticeable

- Ex. Charisma = Confidence + Humor + Good Listening

The most charismatic people in any room are those who make the experience of getting to know them special. They accept who they are; hence, they are comfortable in their own skin. They are confident. They are open-minded. They are positive people who are able to laugh at themselves and share their humor with others. Most of all, they know when to talk and when to listen, so that a natural rhythm to their conversational exchange is achieved seemingly without effort.

In the beginning, you may not be able to be charismatic all of the time; however, charisma is a wonderful goal for anyone who wants to succeed at networking.

***If you lack self-esteem, it's important that you acknowledge this in yourself BEFORE you take on the task of initiating business relationships, so you can do something to gain confidence and be on your way. Remind yourself that you are enough, smile, breath, and take things one step at a time. When you live in the moment, you will not be tripped up by "what might happen" or "what just happened" because you will be operating with all five senses and comforted by the fact that while you are unique, you are still human and one of the tribe.*

MAKE EYE CONTACT

- It's easier to do if you ask yourself, what's the color of his/her eyes?

    - Ex. Look up from the floor.

    Very often your nerves tend to get the best of you when you are put into a room surrounded by a large group people you have yet to meet. Someone walks up to you and begins a conversation and your initial eye contact is replaced with a quick shift of focus to that carpet pattern on the floor. It's as if the floor has become an eye-magnet.

If you do nothing else in this book, break this nervous habit!

Eye contact is a gateway to connecting with people. Ask yourself what is the color of the person's eyes with whom you are speaking. Be sure you know the answer and then check your answer by continuing to make eye contact. It's a way to show interest, to exhibit personal confidence and insure better listening on both your parts.

- Note: every new contact is a friend or ally waiting to be identified

- *Ex. Every friendship you've ever enjoyed began with eye contact.*

At some point in your life, you crossed the frontier of personal interaction by making good eye contact. Whether you forced yourself to make eye contact or it came natural to you, makes no difference. The point is eye contact is the most important connection you can make with a person before you really know who they are. Refrain from the sexy come-hither stare; maintain business-appropriate eye contact and you will make connections with those people that you hope will become valued contacts, clients, and friends.

SPEAK IN SOUND BITES

- Be clear and concise

    - Ex. Tap into the magic of the sound bite.

    When you are meeting people for the first time, it's important to not take all of the "air time." The magic of the sound bite refers to expressing ourselves simply and easily using just a few sentences. This technique allows your listener to remain attentive and to be more likely to want to exchange ideas with you.

- It leaves listeners wanting to hear more, not less

  - Ex. Count on the popularity of the "elevator pitch."

  In the film industry, the sound bite best employed by an aspiring actor or director is called the "elevator pitch." He or she has to be able to convey his or her vision in 1 to 3 terrific sentences. Much can be accomplished in networking by emulating this tactic.

  Boil down the essentials of your subject – say, the nature of your company, your business objectives, or the scope of a proposed project – then speak your summary with confidence. This approach allows your listener to better imprint the vital details and to respond, if interested, with a curiosity to learn more.

- Here's how to achieve a great "sound bite" and/or "elevator pitch"

    - Begin that "great story" in the middle, you can always provide the prologue later.

- Careful repetition of key points empowers the comprehension and memory of your listener.

- Allow a variance in the pitch, expression, and pacing of your voice.

- Once you complete a sound bite, *always* leave air space for your listener to fill with his or her own questions or comments.

LISTEN CAREFULLY

- Often times it's what's between the lines that makes all of the difference

    - Ex. The intonation of a person's voice can give many different meanings to the same words.

Take the word, "hello" for example; it can be a cheerful greeting, or a sarcastic barb depending on the tone of voice of the person saying it. When we are among family or long-time friends, we are often quick to pick up on the subtleties of speech. In a networking situation, however, if you are preoccupied with your objective to make a connection to someone, you may be prone to overlook these verbal innuendos.

It pays to be present, in the moment, when speaking to someone regardless if this is your first conversation with them or the latest in a series. When we listen with *all* of our five senses, we learn more about the subject matter, but more importantly, we learn even more about the character and personality of the individual.

- Observe body language and overall behavior

  - Ex. Is your listener maintaining eye contact, distracted, standing defiantly?

Many books have been written on the subject of body language and how it reflects what we are thinking, or that which we hope to project that we are thinking. Therefore, in networking, it is important to take in the visual cues of your listener. If their body position is mirroring your stance and their head is tilted slightly to one side with a pleasant facial expression, you may conclude that things are going well.

If, however, they appear to be scanning the room with their eyes, tapping their foot, or closing themselves off with crossed arms; it's time to change your approach. It may even be time to cut the conversation short, walk away, and revisit them later. Better to keep them wanting more, than to have them solidify a negative attitude towards you and, equally as important, the company you represent.

- Be aware of your surroundings and peripheral elements/distractions

    - Ex. Standing next to an open microphone is not the place to discuss delicate business.

I cannot tell you how many times that I have had someone strike up a conversation with me while standing under a harsh spotlight in a crowded room, or try to discuss details on a delicate business deal next to an open microphone, or try to make a key point over the loud hub-hub of an enthusiastic networking crowd, then fail to notice the futility of trying to achieve a successful conversation in such a place. It shows a lack of awareness of space, a lack of compassion for your listener, and a lack of professionalism.

Try to adjust as best you can in challenging conversational circumstances. Whenever possible, suggest that you and your listener move to a more appropriate spot in the room. Be mindful in your approach; however, so as not to give the impression that you wish to transform the level of your present business conversation into one more personal in nature.

Simply cite the distraction and collaborate with your listener on selecting a better place to talk.

TAKE NOTE

- When speaking, adjust yourself accordingly to the pace of your listener

    - Ex. Not every listener is willing to jump up to catch the runaway train.

When you find yourself speaking a mile-a-minute, please try to slow down. It's very important for 2 reasons: (1) you will no longer be perceived as being nervous by your listener, and (2) your thoughts will land rather than be gone with the wind.

A better approach is to adjust

The Network Field Guide™

your speech to the pace of your listener. Emulate their speaking rhythms or ask an occasional question to elicit feedback and let you discover just how much has registered. These techniques, done with subtlety, can make you a master at keeping the exchange going.

- Note select details on the back of the business card to spark your memory

    - Ex. Stack the business cards in a pocket or purse in the order that you received them.

Immediately, after the event, pull out the business cards you've collected and note a few key facts on the back. Usually, the name of the event and the date are the most helpful in sparking your memory. However, if there was a key point made or question about which you agreed to follow up, make sure to write it down.

You can choose to note some information at the event itself, but be sure to let your listener know why it is you are writing while listening. A simple, "Let me make a note of this point, right now," will do nicely.

BE A TEAM PLAYER

- Make the conversation an interactive experience

    - Ex. Great repartee requires a little give and take.

    Playwright William Shakespeare was a master at conversational repartee. Some of the most memorable scenes from his plays are because of the rhythmic exchange of thoughts in a linguistic wordplay. We can learn from his examples. While I am not suggesting you speak in iambic pentameter, I am suggesting that you achieve a

The Network Field Guide™

comfortable conversational rhythm, periodically allowing others to express their ideas and receive feedback. Make it a more even exchange and you will create an interactive experience that will leave your listeners wanting more.

- Refrain from enjoying the spotlight for too long an interval

    - Ex. Hollywood starlets captured by the paparazzi.

    How many times have we heard about a starlet's latest escapade ad nauseam? Who cares! I think it is fair to say such publicity seekers quickly suffer from over-exposure from occupying the spotlight of their celebrity too long. We can learn from their example as well: too much is too much. It's much more engaging to periodically showcase others as the center of attention in your conversations.

- Network with a colleague or business associate as your "wing man"

    - Ex. Align yourself with a business colleague whose

skills/services complement those of you and your company and network together.

Years ago, perhaps my most successful networking strategy was to team up with a business colleague who was a natural at making connections. We agreed to introduce each other to whomever one of us happened to be talking to at a given event. If either of us had purchased a table at a function, we helped each other fill it. Through this approach we doubled our respective networks almost immediately.

Our networks kept on growing as people we had connected with through our alliance began to align themselves with us in a similar fashion. Our networks expanded exponentially and within a very short period of time. People began to think of us first when they were in need of information or introductions.

To this day, I feel that the choice to regularly team up has been one of the most beneficial decisions I have made in business. It can work for you too.

FOLLOW UP!

- Do what you say!

    - Ex. If you say, you'll call… CALL!

   We have all been guilty of well-meaning intentions, but how many of us can say that we can pride ourselves on flawless follow-through. Truth is, we try. If you can take your level of follow-through up a level to where you actually do complete the task you promised, you are more likely to be forgiven if there is an instance where you inadvertently drop the ball.

Following through with a new contact is an indication of your level of interest in keeping up a connection and building a good working relationship. It is a preview of what it will be like to work with you and your company. If you know you might have trouble following up on discussions, you will be much better off collecting fewer names or business cards at a function.

- Drop a note about an item of interest where appropriate

- Ex. Send a contact an article which underscores a topic you've recently discussed.

If you have recently spent an hour connecting with someone at a business event on the new LEED standards in architecture, it would be fitting to send an article on the topic that you have come across in a trade journal. It is just another way of keeping in touch. While it is possible that he or she may have already seen it, your thoughtful gesture will be still appreciated.

This is not to say you should

continue peppering your recent contacts with articles in the mail or sign them up for online newsletters simply to remain top-of-mind. Such overzealous efforts will likely backfire. While you may find yourself top-of-mind, you may also move to the top of their proverbial list.

- Think connections and assist your network in making new ones

    - Ex. Become a conduit of information and introductions.

One of the most complimentary aspects of my networking life in business was the fact many of my contacts would call me first when in need of information. Regardless of the topic, they had a confidence in me that I could be helpful. If I had the answer, they knew that I would surely share it. If I didn't know the answer, they knew that I would know of where he or she might find it.

True, I am not walking search engine. My clients called me because they value my ability and willingness to connect people to information, to exchange ideas and to position them for success.

Keep an open-mind and generous nature about your network and it will continue to serve you and your contacts well into the future.

The Network Field Guide™

ARE YOU READY FOR A LITTLE MORE?

Read on…

MORE NETWORKING TIPS

11. **TAKE ONE STEP BACK**
    a. If you're not good at telling jokes, now's NOT the time to try
    b. If you forget someone's name, be honest, warm, and upfront

12. **AVOID THE GRAVITY POCKET**
    a. Notice when things begin to spill, fall, break…and move
    b. Maybe a glass hitting the floor, etc. is a "divine" signal that

it's time to leave

13. **MATCH YOUR COLORS**
    a. If wine is your choice of beverage, take care to notice what might look best against your wardrobe

14. **STAY ON-TRACK**
    a. Don't let a little spill or mishap unsettle you, be unflappable
    b. It pays to be self-effacing

15. **HAVE FUN**
    a. Meeting people should be a joy, so look for it

b. Enjoy the process and you will soon be surrounded by people wanting to get to know you

The Network Field Guide™

TAKE ONE STEP BACK

- If you're not good at telling jokes, now's NOT the time to try

    - Ex. I know you already know someone who's made this faux paux.

    You only have to make this mistake once to promise yourself not to make it again. Even the best jokes can sink you if you fail to properly identify the likes and dislikes of your listener. Therefore, when in doubt, don't!

- Try not to stand too close, too soon

When meeting someone for the first time, be careful not to stand too close. Usually, a distance of about 2 to 3 feet from one another will create a nice comfort zone for your conversation.

- If you forget someone's name, be honest, warm, and upfront

    - Ex. I really want to remember your name, will you repeat it for me, please.

    This is perhaps one of the simplest ways to get over an inability to remember names. Sometimes, you simply cannot remember a name. It just sits there on the tip of your tongue without budging. Resist the urge to be coy, to say the wrong name at the risk of offending this person, or to idle nervously hoping someone will utter it for you. Just swallow your pride and speak the words I have phrased for you on the preceding page. You will solve your problem and make him or her feel a little more comfortable as well.

AVOID THE GRAVITY POCKET

- Notice when things begin to spill, fall, break…and move

    - Ex. If that cup of coffee that just crashed to the floor was a near miss…MOVE!

Whenever things begin to hit the floor, it seems other objects follow, especially when liquids are involved. I have attended events where the same spot has claimed cell-phones, coffee, name tags, and the innocent bystander. Once you notice a tendency for things to spill near you, it's always best to move rather than run the risk that you may be engulfed by it.

- Maybe a glass hitting the floor, etc. is a "divine" signal that it's time to leave

    - Ex. When the spills start, be they mine or someone else's, it's my cue to leave.

This is one of my favorite rules for networking. Since you never want to be that person in the room, who's had a little too much to drink, who fails to keep their wine in their glass, or who gets drenched by someone's beer. Better to leave once it starts. Chances are you missed the first spill, so why risk being on the receiving end of the next one.

Rarely, will you miss anything important at an event where spills are beginning to take center stage. Usually, these mishaps tend to occur a bit later in the program schedule. Therefore, I prefer to think of these mishaps as a timely signal to me that key networking opportunities have passed and it is time to head home.

Not only will your clothes be

dry, your reputation for professionalism will be intact and you will be a welcome sight at the next function.

MATCH YOUR COLORS

- If wine is your choice of beverage, take care to notice what might look best against your wardrobe

    - Ex. Particularly for women, select white wine for light clothing & red wine for dark colors.

    As I mentioned in AVOID THE GRAVITY POCKET, things have a tendency to spill when there are a lot of people crowded into limited space with the objective to network with one another. Rather than have the anxiety of staining your favorite suit with a glass of wine, think ahead about the types of beverages likely to be served and dress to coordinate. Then, if you do experience a spill, you will be less likely to overreact or become angry at the offender. This is especially helpful if the offender turns out to be one of your key contacts.

- If you tend to spill things, take precautions

    - Ex. Keep your glass half full.

You can make things easier on

yourself if you have a tendency to spill things at networking functions. The first is obvious: don't over do it. The second is to choose a non-alcoholic beverage like club soda or ginger ale. Or, third, simply ask the bar tender to give you a light pour in place of a full glass of wine. Fill your wine glass or coffee cup halfway and return for more should you need it. Or, skip the drinks altogether.

If you keep in mind your goal of effective networking, having a cup of coffee or a cocktail becomes much less important.

STAY ON TRACK

- Don't let that spill or mishap unsettle you, be unflappable

    - Ex. Wow! I guess I needed a warm up.

    Okay, it is embarrassing: a cup of coffee has just found its way to your suit. It's hot, you know it and the offender knows it, so why make a big deal of it. If it hurts, say "Ouch", excuse yourself and get medical attention if necessary. If, like most silly spills at networking functions, you were just grazed, take the higher road:

i. Make light of it
   ii. Dust yourself off
   iii. Resume your networking, or simply make a gracious exit

People will remember your graciousness and you will live to network another day.

- It pays to be self-effacing

  - Ex. When you mispronounce a word or misspeak; correct yourself.

People love it when you appear human. There is nothing more distracting from getting to really know someone as when they make an obvious mistake, you can see that they have realized it, and they keep talking as if it never happened. It makes you wonder what else he or she might just glance over with you. Better to own up to your mistakes with a quick correction. It lets everyone move forward together.

HAVE FUN

- Meeting people should be a joy, so look for it

    - Ex. Bring the fresh air in the room, don't be the one sucking the oxygen out of it.

Before you begin to network, take a minute and ask yourself this question,

> *What do I bring to the table?*

It is an important question. When answering it for yourself,

The Network Field Guide™

note your skills, the insights you have on the topic of the moment, and aspects of your personality that might elicit an enthusiastic response to what you have to share.

Now, ask yourself this second question,

> *What makes the people I hope to meet unique and interesting?*

Your answer to this question is perhaps more important than the first one. Why? Because now your focus will be on the people with which you hope to connect. It will no longer be a selfish pursuit. By focusing on your contacts, you will discover what makes them feel comfortable, successful, even happy; and that will make the exercise of building your network authentic and fun.

- Enjoy the process and you will soon be surrounded by people wanting to get to know you

    - Ex. Dare to walk the walk.

Sharing information is no different than sharing stories about oneself. Whatever you choose to share needs to be conveyed in a concise, easy to understand manner, spoken with the right amount of enthusiasm, and tailored to your audience. Take a moment and observe those people who you feel are the most effective at networking and study them. Each person has a process and there is an art to it. Rest assured, that with practice, you also have the capability of being such an artist.

A FEW MORE WORDS OF WISDOM

If you've got the time…

HOW TO WORK THE ROOM

It's a new arena, and you're feeling a bit unprepared to skate the ice. Don't worry. Trust me. You're not the only one who may be feeling out of his or her comfort zone. Instead of turning on a heel and heading for the door, choosing to head straight for the bar to order up a cup of courage, or hyperventilating; take a few slow, quiet, deep breaths and smile. Now, take to the ice.

Your first steps will take you around the room while you casually take in everything.

In particular, try to notice, which people

in the room seem to be approached most often. It's usually the case that those individuals who are most often approached, are the ones you need to meet.

Another deep breath, smile, and approach him or her with the simple phrase, "I don't believe I have had the pleasure of meeting you, I'm (*your name*)."

You'd be surprised how many people will respond favorably to such an introduction. It's straightforward and refreshing. If the reception is a bit too cold for you, simply excuse yourself and try again elsewhere. Before you know it, you'll have struck up a conversation or two with key contacts and your butterflies will be at peace.

THE 3 MOST POWERFUL WORDS IN GETTING AHEAD:
How Can We…

When you use the phrase, "How can we?" or "How can I?" you become empowered to arrive at a solution that will surprise everyone. These 3 little words propel you out of the box of your own way of thinking and forge bonds between new ideas. This is the genesis of creative thinking.

"How can we…" or "How can I…" averts the negativity brought on by the expressions you so often hear:

"You shouldn't…"

"You mustn't…"

"You can't…"

Negative phrases are merely indicative of a self-limiting thought process.

By taking a more expansive tact, you allow fresh thinking and the air in the room increases with the enthusiasm of creativity.

New levels of success are often not far behind.

BE THE BALL

Let yourself enjoy the moment. Just like Chevy Chase's character advises his protégé in *Caddyshack* to "be the ball," we should allow ourselves to be *fully present* and *in the moment* when we network.

By being present, we present the best version of ourselves.

We are actively engaged in the conversational exchange, we are fully aware of our surroundings, and we are listening to what is being said out loud and between the lines.

Being present is to be actively listening, focusing, and taking stock of what is being said as well as how all of it is making us feel.

Rather than looking over our shoulder and mentally checking out to other tasks we might be attending or thinking about a previous conversation, maintain eye contact and listen carefully.

To "be the ball," you have to tune out all of the peripheral noise and concentrate on one specific goal: to make a solid connection. It clears your mind of any irrelevant fleeting thoughts so you can soar.

THE "WIN-WIN"

Strive for the "Win-Win," at every opportunity.

- Win-Win means looking for a way to bring both sides together for a deal that benefits the collective objectives of both parties.

- Win-Win means saving face so that no one feels left out.

- Win-Win means creative and constructive problem solving.

    - Ex. When faced with a problem or quandary for which there is no obvious

> solution, restrain yourself from pointing it out. Challenge yourself to come up with an idea and then revisit the problem later *alongside* your proposed solution.

- Win-Win means exploring the vision and goals of those with whom you are surrounding yourself, identifying synergies, and then acting on them.

- Win-Win means moving forward, adding creativity, energy, and positive outcomes along the way.

- Win-Win means that everyone in the deal gets to feel like the hero at the end of the day.

RISK EXPLORING NEW SUBJECTS

It's surprising the number of people who fail at networking simply because they constantly discuss their firm's line of business without interruption. Imagine trying to learn what motivates these people, if all they do is recite the company brochure.

The old saying, "All work and no play makes Jack a dull boy," rings true.

Granted, an effective business relationship strategy needs to include information about the firm's core business, their strengths and their likely value to a prospective client, but to refrain from discussing any other topic is a quick way to cut off any hope of making a connection.

Businesses, like all areas of our lives, are made up of people, and interesting people make for interesting networking relationships.

By diversifying the subject matter of your networking conversation, you not only discover insights about the type of people that make a particular business tick, you also gain insights into your prospective client's tastes and opinions.

This is useful information when it comes time to convert your initial meeting into that first business opportunity.

The Network Field Guide™

Finding a common ground is the first step to leveling the playing field for you among your competitors.

Background information can speak volumes. It provides a means for you to stay in contact with your new contact in a much less overbearing fashion. Ask yourself, for example, would I prefer to receive numerous brochures from a business contact or a well-timed article on a subject we recently discussed that may or may not arrive accompanied by a company brochure. In the first case, the brochure is likely to hit the infamous FILE # 13, while the second case may even prompt you to lift the phone and say thank you.

In general, a nice mix of topics, none too controversial, will keep the conversation flowing and allow you more face time with the people you need to get to know.

In the weeks following, your attention to their interests in an occasional note or newspaper clipping will keep you top of mind. Keeping connected on multiple levels makes the business connection much more likely to produce pay dirt.

It's okay to talk about subjects other than your line of business, in fact, it can be beneficial. Not only will this approach assist you in cultivating better business relationships, it's a great approach to connecting with people in general.

Let them get to know you and you will get to know them.

GIVERS & TAKERS

When it comes to your own personal energy resources, here are 2 words: protect yourself!

If you are networking and you notice that certain individuals are having a negative effect on your self-confidence, attitude, or demeanor, it's time to take action.

If you let him or her, it is easy to have someone throw you off your game. Many people will try to take the spotlight from you when you're just beginning to get somewhere with an important contact.

> Whether intentional or unintentional, it's important for you to recognize when someone else's behavior is having a negative effect on you.

There is usually no great light that will illuminate above your head; it's more of a feeling of unease that will set over you. Notice it and act quickly.

Perhaps you're in the midst of conversation and someone chooses to enthusiastically disagree with you. You begin to feel attacked. If you defend yourself, you may begin to move from a place of comfort to one of anger; not a good tactic in front of a key contact.

When faced with negativity, the best

approach is to maintain your composure in response to confrontational behavior by simply saying, "That's interesting, why is it you feel so strongly about this?" It allows you to explore their point of view without entering into a spitting contest and shows the key contact that you know how to pick your battles.

Those individuals who always tend to be confrontational or inappropriate in conversation are to be avoided.

Easily minimize your exposure to these people. Simply say, "Will you please excuse me," and slip to the other side of the room. You can always return to your contact later when the coast is clear.

If the negativity is coming from someone with whom you hope to create a beneficial relationship, you need to keep your comments short and sweet.

This illustrates a perfect situation in which a well-timed interaction from a networking partner can speak volumes. It may take a few encounters before you have created a "safe zone" with a negative person. Your partner's warm relationship with the contact can transfer to you if he or she is willing to bring you two together and highlight your strengths to each other.

Depending on your objectives, however, sometimes negativity is simply an obstacle that needs to be avoided.

If someone doesn't like us, it's not always within our power to change it.

Simply move on and avoid this individual altogether. Things will either change or they won't. No matter. There will be plenty of people who will welcome your insights and who will be willing to form rewarding relationships with you.

SOMETIMES IT TAKES A PARTNER

Entering a room with a smile and hand outstretched in greeting not your thing? Don't be afraid to team up.

Effective networking strategists often work together to expand their groups of contacts.

In fact, everyone can use a little help now and then.

Selection of prospective networking partners is critical.

Be especially cognoscente of how you and your partner will be perceived by others.

Females in the business world need to be particularly careful here because of slow-dying stereotypes of male-female relationships.

Professionalism is the key.

Be upfront about your objectives, state your goals clearly, and periodically review the effectiveness of your teaming strategy.

When selling architectural services, my teaming partners included an accountant who catered to real estate developers, commercial bankers, building contractors, land planners, and environmental survey engineers. By meeting with my partners on a regular basis, I was able to learn, track, and act on information well ahead of my competition.

At the core of these partnerships was a trust that any sensitive details would not be revealed without their prior consent.

We simply agreed to introduce each other to anyone new with whom we might be speaking at an event so that our circle of contacts continued to expand.

It's always better to work with a team in my opinion. Many of my former networking partners continue to be my friends. The enlistment of partners to your networking strategy will add balance, humor, and energy to a given event or situation. Plus, it will save you on a day that you're not at your best. Most of all, it makes the business development journey that much more interesting and enjoyable.

Honor your partners and they will honor you.

REGULAR REVIEWS

Go over your networking efforts as soon as you can. For example, if you're attending a luncheon, review your efforts immediately upon returning to your office. It takes just a few minutes and will allow you to record your impressions while they are still fresh in your mind.

Within 24 hours of an event is the best window of time to perform your review.

- Edit out those contacts that were not in keeping with your objectives for attending the event.

The Network Field Guide™

- **Determine which connections matter** the most within the parameters of your goals and objectives and set them aside for timely follow up and easy reference.

- **Promptly following up with a thank you note,** an article of interest or a brochure will be paramount to cultivating these important relationships.

- **Note items of interest** on the back of a business card or in your contact file. They may include:
    - Event information, date, time, venue

- Physical description of the contact to spark your memory
 - Areas of interest, both business-related and otherwise
 - Proposed future projects
 - Pre-existing client relationships
 - Budget considerations

- It's also a good idea to take stock of yourself:
  - Personal strengths and weaknesses
  - Good moments
  - Bad moments
  - Comfort level

- o   Event strategy versus it's perceived outcome

- Consider everything in aggregate, learn from it, make adjustments to your approach where necessary, and move on. It's time to prepare for your next outing.

With regular reviews you will continue to refine your networking prowess and improve your results.

NEXT TIME

There is a quiet, cool confidence when you know and trust that there will be a "next time." Perhaps it is a new construction project, a new committee, or new opportunity to meet a key individual.

To trust in the "next time" is to put trust in you.

Be well aware of your personal value and equity of personality and skill sets; take comfort in knowing that it will all work out.

As Americans, we are taught from an early age to compete. We are taught to seize a given opportunity because there may not be a second chance.

Chances are, if we lay the right groundwork of fundamental skills, there will be a next time, every time.

Keeping this thought in mind eliminates the desperation that often gets expressed as frustration or resentment over small setbacks.

The key to guaranteeing a "next time" is to make each encounter with a contact special and memorable.

Not anything over the top, just a little affinity. Listening well will ensure that a connection is made and acknowledged.

In the meantime, these initial connections multiply in our absence through the connections of all of our contacts to each other.

Eventually, these connections come full circle bringing about the bonus of a "next time" to meet the one person you missed at a given event. Just like magic, you will be standing next to them in a buffet line, seated together at a table, or introduced to them by a networking partner.

The Network Field Guide™

M.I.B. – YOU'RE BOOKED!

M.I.B. is my way of saying, "Money in the bank!" Your list of contacts gleaned through effective networking becomes your savings plan. Make regular deposits, balance the account on a regular basis, and you will be sure to have something there for withdrawal when the time comes.

- Consider the Contact List (or Book) that you are creating as deposits in a money market account.

- You can only make future withdrawals if you have

consistently made regular deposits in the past.

- If you are not seeing any business, go to your Book and begin making calls. Check-in and reconnect. You will be surprised at the number of people who will be delighted to hear from you.

    - Ex. Holidays are always a good time to check in with your contacts by automatically providing a non-business reason to call them that is relevant to both of you. Don't be surprised if

your client surprises
you with a new project
simply because your
call reminded them that
your expertise would be
suited to the work.

AVOID THE QUICKSAND

When commissioned with the task of business development, you are invited to many wonderful and exciting events.

You may think to yourself, I really think my friends or family would really enjoy themselves. Of course, I should bring them along, right? Wrong.

It is such an easy mistake to make when first entering the realm of business networking to expect that your friends and family would be interested or even welcome. In reality, more often than not, it is a bad idea. Why? There is the tendency to divert your focus from your primary objective: creating a rapport for your firm by making strategic connections. Instead, you find yourself taking care of your "guests."

Unless the evening is a black tie or it is the occasional annual luncheon for a large philanthropic organization, bringing along a spouse or partner is usually not appropriate. It is not that people are not curious to know with whom you share your life or that you have nice friends. Rather, it is the tendency of all of us to want to keep our loved ones comfortable, thereby producing an unwelcome distraction.

With loved ones around, we automatically begin to act as hosts. We are obliged to introduce them to everyone we meet, to include them in the conversation, to make sure they have a drink, enough to eat, or a chair. All of these polite pleasantries are appropriate at a dinner, a party, or an evening on the town; but business functions should always have the underlying focus remain on business.

These personal relationships have a tendency to disrespect the business aspect of the function by putting us in a social frame of mind.

While you worry about whether the remark you just made ticked off your spouse, you are not thinking about or listening to the business contact with whom you have worked so hard to earn "face time." In turn, your contact cannot help but form opinions about you from observing how you and your spouse are interacting. All is usually well, if things are good. What tends to occur, more often than not, is that your spouse shows disinterest and may even signal to cut the conversation short, creating a tension you simply do not need.

Now, this is not a license to fool around at business functions.

Being disrespectful of your personal commitments in public usually gets noticed and can undermine all your best efforts to cultivate a trusting business relationship. So, tread carefully. My motto is to keep my business as business and to set aside my social time.

If I decide that a social outing with business contacts and their spouses might be appropriate, I create a specific event to do so.

For example, I will purchase a table at an appropriate gala or host a dinner party at a restaurant where spouses and partners are encouraged to attend.

In short, if you choose to invite friends and family to tag along at a business engagement, you cannot be surprised to find your feet stuck in quicksand… and sinking fast.

FORGIVE YOURSELF

Someone once said, "Life is what happens while you're making other plans." This is true for everything and the sooner you accept it the better off your life will be. Applied to this Networking Field Guide™, this is an anecdote that explains why you will need to forgive yourself every once in awhile simply for being human. You may try my approach and decide it stinks, only to realize you never put your heart into it. Or, you may forget to follow up with that key contact.

You likely have good intentions and hope to earn high marks on everything you set out to do. Some of you will and some of you will not. That being said, I am here to tell you that as long as you keep at it, you will have some success.

If you fail to do something, be sure to acknowledge the failure to yourself. It is feedback after all. Make amends if possible. Forgive yourself, and move forward.

Most of all, though, forgive you.

You must resist the tendency to beat yourself up. Likewise, you must resist the tendency to tell yourself that you will be perfect from now on. Come on, no one is perfect. Besides, perfectionism can easily get out of hand and create its own set of problems and frustrations.

Save the Oscar-winning dives into self-pity for the actors on the silver screen.

If you are at all like me, you are your own harshest critic.

You will not get anywhere in this world without making a mistake, disappointing yourself or someone else. You will make a promise that you will fail to keep, you will get something wrong, and you will, at some point, fail to see what is plainly obvious every now and again. So, get ready to learn form these little foibles because they are the pebbles on the road to your success. For once, give yourself a break, forgive and heal.

Make a mistake. Acknowledge it. Correct it if you can. Learn from it. Forgive yourself. Move on.

Got it? Good!

LIFE-SAVERS**

A few suggestions to keep you at your very best:

- Hard Candy – candy for those of you who like to fidget

- Mints – Always keep a few handy to ensure your breath is fresh

- Hand Lotion – Smooth hands make for a better handshake. Just be sure to put the lotion on well ahead of the event so that your palms are not greasy

The Network Field Guide™

- Fabric Softener Sheets – They tame fly-aways, and dispel static

- Facial Tissues - Offering a spare tissue can initiate a lot of conversations, not to mention, they come in handy

- Lip Balm – Smooth lips show you care about yourself at the most basic level

- Manicure – Well-kept hands show seriousness about being respected by others

- Antibacterial Lotion – Great way to prevent flu by keeping your hands germ-free. Best applied in the privacy of a restroom rather than in public

- Quarters – You will be the hero of the day when you can easily produce one for a contact's parking meter or vending machine

- Dollar Bills – Keep a few on hand for tipping the parking valet, doorman, coat check, bar tender, etc., at business events

- Baby Wipes – Keep a travel-size pack in your desk drawer or car trunk. Wipes are wizards at removing spills and stains from clothing, usually without leaving a residue when the area dries. Great to use to freshen up on a hot day, too

- Dental Floss - a pocket tin of floss helps you to avoid the embarrassing sesame seed or spinach between your teeth moment

**You may be inclined to think that these items only apply to females; I assure you they can aid members of both sexes. You need not carry a handbag in lieu of a billfold, but a well-stocked office drawer or car trunk will quickly earn its keep.

AFTER WORDS…

EPILOGUE

I hope this book has helped you. Networking has become a way of life with me. I see synergies in everything and the more I connect with people and help them to connect with each other, the better I feel. It's a small planet, so why not get to know one another better? We all want to be successful at something.

We each possess a personal strength or special gift.

I have made it my mission to assist those I meet along the way with expressing the best of themselves.

When done honestly, it's anything but schmoozing. There is a primary difference, in my mind, between someone who *networks* and someone who *schmoozes*.

People who network with one another care about the people with whom they connect and hope to build long-term relationships.

Schmoozers tend to indulge in the thrill of the momentary association, and afterwards, they couldn't care less. An effective *Networker* follows up on his or her promises, strives to position all parties for success, and is honest about his or her ability to deliver on those promises.

Honor those individuals with whom you hope to connect.

Networking really is that simple.

ACKNOWLEDGEMENTS

My sincere thanks to my family and friends who have supported me through the process of writing this field guide including but not limited to: Sonya Boone of the American Medical Association; Jana Schreuder, Kathleen Soto, and Angela West of Northern Trust; and Ken Selzer of Aon and, more importantly, the USC Marshall School of Business Alumni Association. I would like to express my gratitude to the late John Hench and the late Peggy Van Pelt of Walt Disney Imagineering; Gerry Gilmore of Hellmuth, Obata & Kassabaum, Inc.; Tolbert Chisum of Wintrust Financial; Dan Sullivan of Gensler, Inc.; Robert A. Helman, former

Chairman of Mayer Brown; Jim Reynolds of Loop Capital; Robert Labate of Holland and Knight; and Les Coney of Mesirow Financial.

In addition, I would like to thank Howard W. Melton, my attorney and dear friend, who spent countless hours reviewing this manuscript and holding me to a deadline. It follows that I should also express a special thank you to the late John Calloway of WTTW/PBS Chicago who not only encouraged my writing, but helped me to reframe the setbacks in my life as unique opportunities to further express my creativity. Without Howard and John, this book would probably never have happened.

Thank you to my little angel of a puppy whose insistence on a belly rub, walk or pick-up game of fetch helped me to pace myself and maintain my sanity.

To the man in my life, I give a heartfelt thank you. Your unconditional love and supportive nature puts a smile on my face every day and enables me to rest peacefully every night.

In closing, to the terrific production team of individuals who transformed this project from vision to reality: well done.

AUTHOR'S PORTRAIT
Terry Frick Photography
Los Angeles, CA

ABOUT THE AUTHOR

Kathy Corday is a native of Los Angeles where she graduated from the University of Southern California Marshall School of Business and attended the USC School of International Relations as a Herman Fellow. Her multi-faceted career includes television host for PBS national and regional programs, business development director for the Chicago office of the architecture firm of Hellmuth Obata & Kassabaum (HOK), and award-winning photographer for both Walt Disney Imagineering and the National Museum of African Art at the Smithsonian. Ms. Corday lives in Chicago and is an active member of SAG, AFTRA and AEA, as well as a variety of civic and professional organizations.

The Network Field Guide™

ON THE HORIZON...

Ms. Corday is readying additional original works for publication including: the children's book *The Flower Gift,* the morality fable, *Gray,* and a collection of essays examining the labyrinth of single life in Chicago's windy city, *The Flirting Class: Diving Deep into the Pool of Life.*

The Network Field Guide™

Copyright © 2007 Kathy Corday

Thank you for purchasing The Networking Field Guide™: Essential Social Skills for Business. I wish you the best of luck in all of your networking endeavors.

-KC-

NOTES

Printed at Grace Printing, Chicago, Illinois, USA

ISBN: 978-0-9843897-0-4